FINANCIAL AND WHEALTHY CLAIMS

FINANCIAL AND WHEALTHY CLAIMS

# FINANCIAL AND WEALTHY CLAIMS

## THE GREAT BOOK OF POWERFUL CLAIMS AND PHRASES FROM FINANCIAL GURUS!

FINANCIAL AND WHEALTHY CLAIMS

# INDEX

Introduction

Chapter 1: What about financial and wealth claims

Chapter 2: Financial Quotes

Chapter 3: General financial statements

Chapter 4: Financial Citations in Investment

Chapter 5: Conclusion

FINANCIAL AND WHEALTHY CLAIMS

# Introduction

Many people are looking to earn more income, increase their wealth, become debt-free and financially secure. Many individuals wonder why a few individuals are blessed with much income and others are not. Well, there are many mysteries in life, however a principle that is as old as the ages, is the Law of Attraction. Get all the information you need here.

# Chapter 1: What about financial and wealth claims

What is the law of attraction? It has become an increasingly popular viral word since the wild fame of books like "The Secret" and the movie "The Secret".

However, long before "The Secret", individuals have been using positive affirmations and visualization to attract the things they desire into their lives.

The principle is quite simple. Essentially, the Law of Attraction says that whatever you are thinking or feeling manifests in your life.

For example, have you ever thought about an old acquaintance you haven't talked to in a long time? You question what they're doing, and suddenly someone starts talking about them, or they appear in your life in some crazy way - you add yourself as a friend on Facebook, for example.

**That's how the Law of Attraction works.**

We have thousands of thoughts running through our brains every day, and the crucial thing is to fine-tune and focus those thoughts and feelings on what we want, so that what we want appears!

FINANCIAL AND WHEALTHY CLAIMS

The reason most individuals don't earn income, or don't find income easy to earn, is because they have harmful associations and notions about income.

If you think that income makes you vicious, or that income is difficult to acquire, or that anyone who has income must have swindled someone, or that individuals who have income are selfish, then naturally, you are not going to attract prosperity into your life. If you are constantly focused on your debt, you will always be in debt.

When you begin to focus on income as a simple energy that can flow easily into your life, you will be surprised how easily it does. Affirmations can help shape your thoughts and feelings about income, so you will begin to alter your notions and get more income.

# FINANCIAL AND WHEALTHY CLAIMS

It is crucial that your income affirmations are credible to you. If you resist them, you will not be effective in attracting wealth and earning income. So if claiming an affirmation like "I'll make a million dollars this year" doesn't feel like something that's feasible, it won't show up, even when you claim it.

In this book there are income statements and income quotes that I have used in the past and in the here and now that are helping me to make income, to get income, and to have free income simply appear in my life.

It is crucial to authentically feel true gratitude for whatever you are given. Gratitude is one of the keys to happiness, and to prosperity.

## FINANCIAL AND WHEALTHY CLAIMS

The illustration, "I want to be in a satisfying relationship for life" and "I don't want to end up sad and alone" may seem like two ways of saying the same thing. They are not. To your subconscious mind, they are saying the opposite.

Your subconscious mind doesn't understand the difference between "I wish" and "I don't wish. It simply hears "fulfilling relationship for life" or "sad and lonely.

If you want to master your affirmation to produce the wealth and prosperity you desire, you have to do it right.

Although the positive affirmations come in many forms, the structure remains the same. Whatever form you choose, be as clear,

FINANCIAL AND WHEALTHY CLAIMS

particular and precise as possible:

**I am:** An affirmation of who you are.

These are positive affirmations of a true state of being that lives within you. You can achieve a complete list of "I am" affirmations by making a favorable personal inventory of your attributes, strengths, talents and competencies.

- I am perfectly healthy in mind, body and spirit.
- I am a master mind and use my wisdom every day.
- I am passionate about everything I work for.

FINANCIAL AND WHEALTHY CLAIMS

**I can do it:** A statement of your potential.

This is a favorable expression of your power to achieve goals. It is a statement of your confidence in your power to grow, change and help yourself.

I can" statements can be designed after you have a set of goals.

- I can love my partner unconditionally.
- I can quit smoking easily.
- I can grow my business and be financially free.

**I will do it:** A statement of favorable change in your life.

FINANCIAL AND WHEALTHY CLAIMS

Favorable statements of what you want to happen. A prophecy of success. Affirmations of my will are made after you have established your priorities and goals. Many times the word "will" can be removed to bring the statement into the here and now.

- I will love and nurture myself better each day.
- I'll gain more confidence every day.
- I will do my visualizations every day.

FINANCIAL AND WHEALTHY CLAIMS

# Chapter 2: Financial Quotes

Financial and wealth quotes can inspire you. Let's take a look at some.

**Quotes**

- "Women fake orgasms and men fake finances." - Suze Orman

- "If you're in the luckiest one of humanity, you owe it to the rest of humanity to think about the other 99 percent."-

Warren Buffett

## FINANCIAL AND WHEALTHY CLAIMS

- "Rule No. 1: Never lose money. Rule No. 2: Never forget Rule No. 1. - Warren Buffett

- "A man always has two reasons for what he does... a good one, and the real one." - J.P. Morgan

- "I try not to borrow, first you borrow, then you beg." - Ernest Hemingway

- "Forecasts can tell you a lot about the prognosticator; they don't tell you anything about the future." - Warren Buffett

- "People of the same trade rarely meet, even for fun, but the conversation ends in a conspiracy against the public, or in some

## FINANCIAL AND WHEALTHY CLAIMS

artifice to raise prices" - Adam Smith, The Wealth of Nations: An investigation into the nature and causes of the wealth of nations

- "Your actions are your only true possessions." - Allan Lokos, Patience: The art of peaceful living.

- "This story is the latest example of America's greatest political problem. We no longer have the attention span to deal with any crisis of the 21st century. We live in an immensely complex economy and are completely at the mercy of the small group of people who understand it - who, by the way, often happen to be the same people who built these wildly complex economic systems. We have to trust these people to do the right thing, but we cannot, because, well, they are scum. This is a big problem, if you think about it. Matt Taibbi, Griftopia: Bubble machines, vampire squid and the long con that's tearing America apart.


- "Our moral economy went bankrupt long before the financial one." Steve Maraboli, No Apologies: Reflections on Life and the Human Experience.


- "The basic scam in the Internet age is fairly easy to understand even for the financially illiterate. It was like banks like Goldman wrapping ribbons around watermelons, throwing them out fifteen-story windows, and opening the phones to make offers. In this game you're only a winner if you get your money out before the melon hits the sidewalk" - Matt Taibbi, Griftopia: Bubble Machines, Vampire Squid, and the Long Con that's Breaking America

# FINANCIAL AND WHEALTHY CLAIMS

- "Price is not just a matter of numbers. It's a satisfying sacrifice."

Toba Beta, Master of Stupidity

- "Businessmen are like sharks, not only because we are grey and a little greasy, or because our teeth follow the trail of the entrails of those we have eviscerated, but because we must advance or die."

Stanley Bing

- "No one should abandon a woman after throwing a lot of gold at her in her distress! He should love her forever! You are young, only twenty-one, and you are kind and upright and fine.

## FINANCIAL AND WHEALTHY CLAIMS

You will ask me how a woman can accept money from a man. Oh, God, isn't it natural to share everything with the one to whom we owe all our happiness? When one has given everything, how can one argue about a mere portion of it? Money is important only when the feeling has ceased. Isn't one destined for life? How can you foresee separation when you think someone loves you? When a man swears eternal love, how can there be separate concerns in that case?" - Honoré de Balzac, Father Goriot

- "You could still go to some industry or some university or the government and if you could persuade them that you have something at stake, then they could put the money in after cutting themselves off from almost all the profits. And, naturally, they would run the show because it was their money and all you had done was sweat and

 FINANCIAL AND WHEALTHY CLAIMS

bleed." - Clifford D. Simak, All the Traps of Earth

- "In many ways, the effect of the accident on embezzlement was more significant than on suicide. For the economist, embezzlement is the most interesting of crimes. Only among the various forms of theft does it have a time parameter. Weeks, months or years may pass between the commission of the crime and its discovery. (This is a period, by the way, in which the embezzler has his gain and the man who has been embezzled, curiously, feels no loss. There is a net increase in psychic wealth). ) At any given time there is an inventory of undiscovered embezzlement in - or more precisely not in - the country's businesses and banks. This inventory - perhaps it should be called embezzlement - amounts at any given time to many millions of dollars. It also varies in size with the business cycle.

In good times people are relaxed, confident, and money is abundant. But even though money is abundant, there are always many people who need more. Under these circumstances the rate of embezzlement increases, the rate of discovery decreases, and embezzlement increases rapidly. In depression all this is reversed.

Money is watched with a narrow and suspicious eye. The man who handles it is supposed to be dishonest until he proves otherwise. Audits are pervasive and meticulous. Business morality has improved enormously. The bezzle is shrinking. John Kenneth Galbraith

FINANCIAL AND WHEALTHY CLAIMS

- Just as the boom accelerated the rate of growth, crack greatly advanced the rate of discovery. Within days, something close to universal confidence became something close to universal suspicion. Audits were ordered. Tense or troubled behavior was noted. Most importantly, the collapse of stock values made irredeemable the position of the employee who had embezzled to play the market. He now confessed." John Kenneth Galbraith, The Great Shock of 1929

- "Personal finances are like people's personal health, crucial and tragic for the sufferer but tedious for the listener. "- Thomas Keneally, Finding Schindler: A Memory

- "The point of retirement is to live off your assets, not them"...

FINANCIAL AND WHEALTHY CLAIMS

Frank Eberhart

- "The first rule of making money is not to lose it." - Steven J.

Lee, The Money Plan: Creating Personal Wealth for a Secure Future

- "Am I in debt? I'm a true American!" - From "Perfect Strangers"

- "The virtues of free enterprise can be distorted by greed and deception." - Allan Lokos, Patience: The Art of Peaceful Living

- "You won't love your investment adviser, because if she was that smart she'd be retired

FINANCIAL AND WHEALTHY CLAIMS

by now." - Steven J. Lee, The Money Plan: Creating Personal Wealth for a Secure Future

- "You will not forget that money is only money and not character or fame." - Steven J. Lee, The Money Plan: Creating Personal Wealth for a Secure Future

- "I see dead presidents. Lincoln, Jefferson, Franklin and Washington." - Nicole Fende, How to be a financial rock star

- Many small businesses would rather face a horde of angry barbarians than deal with their cash flow situation or price a new product" - Nicole Fende, How to be a Finance Rock Star

## FINANCIAL AND WHEALTHY CLAIMS

- "Well, you see that girl over there, the one in that group who keeps looking at you?"... "Well, let's say I'm convinced she's wearing black panties - she looks like a girl in black panties to me - and I'm so sure that's what she's wearing, so sure of that sartorial fact, that I want to bet a million dollars. The problem is, if I'm wrong, I'm finished. So I also bet that she's wearing panties that aren't black, but any of a whole basket of colors - let's say I put nine hundred and fifty thousand dollars on that possibility: that's the rest of the market; that's the hedge. This is a crude example, all right, in every way, but listens to me. Now, if I am right, I make fifty thousand, but even if I am wrong I am going to lose fifty thousand, because I am covered. And because 95 percent of my million dollars is not in use...

I will never be called upon to prove it: the

only risk is in the spread - I can make similar bets with other people. Or I can bet on something else entirely. And best of all, I don't have to be right all the time - if I can get the color of your underwear right fifty-five percent of the time I'm going to end up very rich..." - Robert Harris, The Fear Index


- "If you owe ten pounds to the Bank of England, they put you in jail, but if you owe a million pounds, they invite you to join the Board" - Philippe Ries


- "The capital accumulated in the 18th and 19th centuries through various forms of the slave economy is still circulating," said De Jong, "continues to attract interest, to increase many times over and to continually flourish again" - W.G. Sebald

 FINANCIAL AND WHEALTHY CLAIMS

# Chapter 3: General financial statements

You are capable of affirming yourself to have great wealth and prosperity. Let's look at some affirmations.

**Affirmations**

- My financial abundance is overflowing today.

- The presence of joy in my heart releases an abundance of good in my life.

## FINANCIAL AND WHEALTHY CLAIMS

- I was destined to be prosperous. I have abundance to share and to save.

- Now I make a fortune doing what I love.

- Money comes easily and freely.

- Now I give and receive more freely.

- Now I attract money effortlessly.

- Now I am a powerful money magnet.

- I immediately respond in faith to the guidance of the Holy Spirit within me. I am always in the right place at the right time

FINANCIAL AND WHEALTHY CLAIMS

because my steps are ordered by the Higher Power.

- The Higher Power has given me all things that pertain to life and godliness, and I am able to possess all that the Higher Power has provided for me.

- Wealth is pouring into my life.

- I will create a home full of joy and peace.

- I am free from debt

- I'm constantly adding to my income

## FINANCIAL AND WHEALTHY CLAIMS

- I'm financially free

- The Higher Power is the unfailing and unlimited source of my supply. My financial income now increases as the blessings of the Higher Power take me.

- I now attract incredible opportunities to increase my wealth and my life.

- I now have worry-free financial freedom in the world!

- I thank God for my financial values.

- I can now invest my money wisely.

## FINANCIAL AND WHEALTHY CLAIMS

- Now I get divine wisdom in money matters.

- I not only receive money, but I also give money.

- Now I attract money easily.

- When I give, I am given, in good measure, squeezed, shaken, and run over. (Please note that giving comes in all forms... money, a helping hand, your time for another, your encouragement, your smile. All you need is the willingness to give for that day, as directed).

- I now earn ($ ) a month.

## FINANCIAL AND WHEALTHY CLAIMS

- I have ($ ) at the end of this week.

- I can now give ($ ) per week/month to the less fortunate.

- My finances are divinely blessed.

- I am now in control of my finances.

- I am like a tree planted by rivers of water, I bear fruit in my time, my leaf does not wither, and everything I do will prosper. The grace of the Higher Power even makes my mistakes prosper.

- I attract opportunities to myself

# FINANCIAL AND WHEALTHY CLAIMS

- I'm a money magnet. I see myself as a billionaire.

- Everything I want comes to me easily and effortlessly.

- I am in the process of attracting a job that will provide financial security for me and my family.

- Wealth is flooding into my family as I speak

- I am prosperous in everything I do

- All obstacles and hindrances to my prosperity have been dissolved.

## FINANCIAL AND WHEALTHY CLAIMS

- I now have complete financial freedom to do, be and have anything I wish.

- Now I am becoming more and more prosperous every day.

- I have a continuous abundance of money flowing to me always

- I am now permanently free of debt and any kind of money problem.

- I always think positively about money.

- I have many financial opportunities.

## FINANCIAL AND WHEALTHY CLAIMS

- I always find a way to make a big profit.

- I am rich and prosperous.

- I have faith that I am being guided in ways that bring amazing results.

- I fill my mind with the idea of abundance, and abundance manifests in all my affairs.

- I recognize my true Source and let prosperity pour into each of my experiences.

- My partner and I take control of our finances and budget on a regular basis.

## FINANCIAL AND WHEALTHY CLAIMS

- I begin today to open myself up to greater and greater prosperity.

-My income is constantly increasing.

- I now receive my good from both expected and unexpected sources.

- I am surrounded by very smart, super effective and brilliant business people...

- Abundance surrounds me. Today I claim my share.

- My thoughts of prosperity create my prosperous world.

# FINANCIAL AND WHEALTHY CLAIMS

- My life is filled with an abundance of goods.

- With the guidance of the Higher Power, my life is full of joyful success and rich abundance.

- I release all feelings of lack and limitation. I accept with joy the blessings of joy and abundance.

- Today it is rich in opportunities and I open my heart to receive them.

- Money flows freely and abundantly in my life.

## FINANCIAL AND WHEALTHY CLAIMS

- Attracting money is easy.

- I am my own boss. I work when I want, where I want, and how I want, and I am paid handsomely for my efforts.

- I am a billionaire.

- Money comes to me easily and effortlessly.

- I am open and receptive to new avenues of income.

- I attract abundance without effort.

- I deserve to be rich.

## FINANCIAL AND WHEALTHY CLAIMS

- Wonderful things happen to me because I live with an attitude of gratitude.

- I am worthy of everything my heart desires. It is my divine heritage!

- I imagine abundance for myself and others.

- I always have more money coming in than going out.

- I allow myself to have more than I ever dreamed possible.

- I fully believe in my ability to attract money.

- I have a money mentality.

## FINANCIAL AND WHEALTHY CLAIMS

- Money always seems to come my way.

- I naturally attract money and material abundance.

- I trust that everything will come at the perfect time and in the perfect way.

- I surrender to my higher good.

- I invite and allow good into my life.

- I provide for myself abundantly as I go on my way.

## FINANCIAL AND WHEALTHY CLAIMS

- I know my value, I honor my value.

- All the money I spend enriches society and returns to me multiplied.

- My life is full of abundance.

- I am focused on achieving wealth.

- My bank account never seems to stop growing.

- I am very focused on achieving financial success.

- I am open to receive.

## FINANCIAL AND WHEALTHY CLAIMS

- I feel good about all the money I spend.

- My money is a source of good for me and others.

- I am financially independent and free.

- I have a large, stable, reliable and permanent financial income now.

- The Higher Power longs to bring me good!

- I am filled with the knowledge of the will of the Higher Power in all wisdom and spiritual understanding, His will is my prosperity.

- I forbid thoughts of failure and defeat to dwell in my mind.

# FINANCIAL AND WHEALTHY CLAIMS

- I am filled with the wisdom of the Higher Power, and I am led to make wise and prosperous financial decisions. The Spirit of the Higher Power guides me into all truth regarding my financial affairs.

- The Higher Power makes my thoughts agree with His will?my plans are set and successful.

- Having received the abundance of grace and the gift of righteousness, I reign as a king in life.

- I always have money.

- I attract financial abundance.

FINANCIAL AND WHEALTHY CLAIMS

- My mind is well tuned to attract massive wealth.

 FINANCIAL AND WHEALTHY CLAIMS

# Chapter 4: Financial Citations in Investment

To have good investment skills, you must have inspiration and knowledge in particular areas. Let's look at quotes from some of these particular areas.

**Skills you need**

- "The individual investor must consistently act as an investor and not as a speculator. - Ben Graham You is an investor, not someone who can anticipate the future. Base your conclusions on true facts and analysis rather than risky and unsafe forecasts.

# FINANCIAL AND WHEALTHY CLAIMS

- "It's not about how much money you make, but how much money you save, how much it costs you and how many generations you save it for. - Robert Kiyosaki

If you're a millionaire in the early years, but lose everything in midlife, you've made a lot of money. Grow and protect your investment portfolio by carefully diversifying it, and you'll find yourself financing many generations to come.

- "Know what you own, and know why you own it." - Peter Lynch Do your homework before you makes a decision. And once you've made a decision, be sure to reevaluate your portfolio in a timely manner. Sensible retention now may not be wise retention

FINANCIAL AND WHEALTHY CLAIMS

later.

- "Financial peace is not the acquisition of things. It's learning to live on less than you earn, so you can pay back the money and have money to invest. You can't earn until you do this." - Dave Ramsey

By being modest in your expenses, you can ensure that you will have enough for your retirement and can give back to the community as well.

- "Investing should be more like watching paint dry or watching grass grow. If you want excitement, take $800 and go to Las Vegas. - Paul Samuelson

## FINANCIAL AND WHEALTHY CLAIMS

If you feel that investing is gambling, you're doing it wrong. The work involved requires planning and patience. Still, the gains you see over time are touching!

- Funds in the investment world don't end with four-year minimums; they end with 10- or 15-year minimums. - Jim Rogers Although ten- or fifteen-year minimums are not typical, they do happen. During these depressing times, don't be shy about going around the curve and investing; you could make a fortune making a move without fear - or lose it all.

- "I'll tell you how to get rich. Close the doors. Be afraid when others are greedy. Be greedy when others are fearful." -

Warren Buffett

## FINANCIAL AND WHEALTHY CLAIMS

Be prepared to invest in a falling market and to "exit" in a rising market.

- "The stock market is full of individuals who know the price of everything, but the value of nothing." - Phillip Fisher A different testament to the fact that investing without training and research will eventually lead to regrettable investment decisions. Research is much more than just listening to public opinion.

- "In investing, what is comfortable is rarely profitable." - Robert Arnott

From time to time, you will have to step outside your comfort zone to make significant gains. Understand the limits of your comfort zone and exercise outside it in small doses. As much as you know the market, you must also know yourself. Can you handle staying in the market when everyone else is retreating? Or going out during the biggest rally of the century? There's no room for pride in this kind of self-analysis. The biggest investment scheme can become the worst if you don't have the stomach to stick with it.

- "How many millionaires do you know who have gotten rich by investing in savings accounts? I have nothing more to say." -

Robert G. Allen

While investing in savings is a safe bet, your earnings will be minimal given the

FINANCIAL AND WHEALTHY CLAIMS

excessively low interest rates. However, don't give up on one completely. A savings account is a reliable place for an emergency fund, while a market investment is not.

- Invest in yourself. Your career is the engine of your wealth. - Paul Clitheroe

We all want wealth, but how do we get it? It starts with a successful career that builds on your talents and skills. Invest in yourself with education, books or a quality job where you can develop a quality skill set. Identify your talents and discover a way to turn them into an income-generating monster. By doing this, you can truly leverage your career on wealth.

- "Every once in a while, the market does something so stupid it takes your breath

# FINANCIAL AND WHEALTHY CLAIMS

away." - Jim Cramer There are no safe bets in the investment arena; there is risk in everything. Be prepared for the ups and downs.

- "I wouldn't pay up front. I'd invest in your place and let the investments cover it. - Dave Ramsey

A perfect answer to the question: "Should I pay my _____ (fill in the blank) or invest for retirement? That said, a 30% credit card balance can become a black hole if not paid promptly. Essentially, pay off debt at high interest rates and keep debt at lower rates.

- "An investment in knowledge pays the best interest." -

 FINANCIAL AND WHEALTHY CLAIMS

# Benjamin Franklin

If it is a question of investment, nothing will pay more than one's schooling. Do the essential research, study and analysis before drawing conclusions about the investment.

- "The four most dangerous words for investment are: "This time it's different. - Sir John Templeton

Follow the trends and history of the market. Don't expect this particular time to be different. For example, an important key to investing in a particular stock or bond fund is its performance over five years.

- "Broad diversification is only necessary

 FINANCIAL AND WHEALTHY CLAIMS

when investors do not understand what they are doing. - Warren Buffett

Originally, diversification is crucial. Once you've got your feet wet and you're confident in your investments, you can adjust your portfolio accordingly and make bigger bets.

- "There are recessions, there are falls in the stock market. If you don't understand that's going to happen, then you're not ready, you won't do well in the markets. - Peter Lynch If you get hit by recessions or declines, you have to stay the course. Economies are cyclical and markets have shown that they will recover.

Be sure to be a part of that!

FINANCIAL AND WHEALTHY CLAIMS

The investment world can be cold and difficult. However, if you research thoroughly and keep your head on straight, your chances of long-term success are convincing. Re-read these quote if you feel shaky or unsettled about investing. How are they relevant to your experience? Do you have any quotes to add?

# Chapter 5: Conclusion

You can intensify your statements with one word: easily.

I'm bringing in a hundred thousand dollars a month versus I'm easily bringing in a hundred thousand dollars a month.

Notice how the word easily brings a sense of calm and intensifies the favorable emotional effect of the affirmation?

Here are some additional ways to make your affirmations more powerful:

## FINANCIAL AND WHEALTHY CLAIMS

Make sure your affirmations are bold, clear and positive.

Practice saying your affirmations for half an hour a day. Say them in your head and out loud, even if it's embarrassing. Your new vision requires courage and you can't wait for your affirmations to seem genuine - they won't seem genuine until you start believing them.

If you begin to question your claims, recognize that your unconscious mind is sending you a signal based on your conditioning - not on what you are capable of achieving.

Continue to recommit to the procedure. Each time you set a higher goal for yourself,

FINANCIAL AND WHEALTHY CLAIMS

dedicate yourself to re-articulating that goal and imprinting it on your unconscious mind.

In addition to your affirmation, take action.

An affirmation will not cause results in your life unless you have the right plan to support that affirmation and are taking daily action according to the plan.

If your desire is to have an abundance of cash to meet your needs, practice this statement for cash: "I always have an abundance of cash to meet all my needs.

Repeat it many times, and then stop affirming. Be silent as you recognize, visualize, and feel what it is like to already

 FINANCIAL AND WHEALTHY CLAIMS

have the amount of money you want.

Feel as if it has already happened, and that all your needs are more than satisfied. While you are in that state, be open to all the ways and means by which you will attract money into your life to meet all your needs.

Choose the affirmations that seem appropriate to you, those that resonate with you, or that appeal to your emotions. It is crucial that the words feel comfortable to you and that they are in line with who you are. Feel free to produce one for your particular need by substituting other words that have special meaning for you.

Remember that affirmations take a little time, however, once you begin the procedure, you

FINANCIAL AND WHEALTHY CLAIMS

will be surprised at how quickly it happens. Initially, it feels like a lot of work without much result, but soon the momentum of the procedure begins to take over.

Inside you, there is a star that wants to express itself. All you have to do is learn how to use your conscious faculties to harness the fantastic power of that unconscious mind of yours.

Finally (read this aloud): I am achieving everything I set out to do.

## SUCCESS AND PROSPERITY!!!!

# FINANCIAL AND WHEALTHY CLAIMS

Visit our author page on Amazon and get more MENTES LIBRES!

http://amazon.com/author/menteslibres

If you wish, you can leave a comment on this book by clicking on the following link so that we can continue to grow! Thank you very much for your purchase!

https://www.amazon.com/dp/B084331ZSH

www.ingramcontent.com/pod-product-compliance
Lightning Source LLC
Chambersburg PA
CBHW050300220526
45465CB00002B/755